Edited by Larry Keltto

ISBN-13: 978-1466381391
ISBN-10: 1466381396

Printed in the United States of America

THE SOLOPRENEUR LIFE

42 Solo-Business Owners Speak the Truth on Dreaming Big, Failing Forward, and Calling Your Own Shots

Edited by Larry Keltto

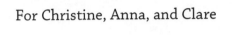
For Christine, Anna, and Clare

Contents

viii. Introduction
ix. Introducing The Solopreneurs

13   Why Did You Start Your Business?

23   What Was the Best Thing You Did
        When Starting Your Business?

35   What Is a Mistake That
        You Have Learned From?

49   What Lifestyle Changes Have You Made
        to Stay In Business?

55   What Are Your Strategies
        For Staying Competitive?

65   What Is Your Biggest Current Challenge?

77   Where Do You Want
        Your Business To Be In Five Years?

85   If Your Business Should Fail,
        What Is Your Fallback Plan?

93   What Is Your Advice For
        Aspiring Solopreneurs?

109   If You Were Starting All Over,
        What Would You Do Differently?

117   Are You Glad You Became a Solopreneur?

131   About the Editor

"It is never too late to be what you might have been."
— George Eliot

Introduction

In April 2010 I began publishing on my Web site (TheSolopreneurLife.com) a weekly Q&A interview with a solopreneur. The purpose of the feature was to learn from how other solopreneurs operate their businesses.

I *thought* the series was a good idea; I *knew* it was good when the first "Featured Soloist" was published and I immediately began receiving inquiries from solopreneurs who were requesting to be featured.

So every Tuesday morning for about a year, I posted "Featured Soloist" on TheSolopreneurLife. com. Along the way, several people suggested that I compile the best advice from the soloists and publish it as a book. That's what I did, and this book is the result.

The solopreneurs featured in these pages come from around the world. Their ages vary greatly. Their level of experience as solopreneurs ranges from "just started" to veteran. They work in different industries. Taken together, their thoughts give us a snapshot of the solopreneur life as it's being experienced in 2010 and 2011 around the world.

My business is stronger for having read the wisdom in "Featured Soloist," and I think it will help you, too.

Acknowledgements

I want to thank all of the solopreneurs who took the time and made the effort to be "Featured Soloists." Special thanks to Barbara Milgram and Laurie Gay, the first ones who said "yes" to being featured.

Thank you to Naomi Niles, who suggested people who would be interesting soloists.

Thank you to Derek Peterson, a longtime friend and a great encourager of TheSolopreneurLife.com.

Thank you to my wife, Christine, who's been my sounding board for all things solopreneur.

Thank you to my daughters, Anna and Clare, who are the reason why I choose the solopreneur life every day.

And thank you to our dog, Griffin, who's always nearby while I work, no matter how late the hour.

—Larry Keltto
September 2011

Introducing
The Solopreneurs

Bob Andelman, Mr. Media Radio Interviews,
St. Petersburg, Florida
Koldo Barroso, Bellingham, Washington
Nichole Bazemore: Simply Stated Solutions, Atlanta
David Billings, Sparky Firepants Images,
Portland, Oregon
Laura Brandenburg, Clear Spring Business Analysis,
Denver, Colorado
Marianne Cantwell, London, England
Jill Chivers, I'm Listening Now, Sunshine Coast,
Queensland, Australia
Heather Claus, 365 Days of Everything,
Wilmington, North Carolina
Patrick Curtis, Wall Street Oasis, Boston
Mel DePaoli, Omicle, Seattle
Melissa Dinwiddie, Mountain View, California
Bill Dwight, FamZoo, Inc., Palo Alto, California
Laurie Gay, BluePrint Balance, Atlanta, Georgia
Tzaddi Gordon, ThriveWire Media, Sunshine Coast,
British Columbia

Deb Howard Greenleaf, Greenleaf Accounting
Services, LLC, Northwestern Pennsylvania
Diana L. Guerrero aka "Ark Lady," DBA as
Ark Animals & Guerrero Ink, offices in
Big Bear Lake, California
Amy Harrison, Harrisonamy Copywriting,
Brighton, United Kingdom
Andy Hayes, Hayes Media Group, Seattle
Dawn Svenson Holland, FlashPoint Fundraising,
Cedar Rapids, Iowa
Sherice Jacob, Charleston, West Virginia
Burton Kelso, Integral Computer Consultants,
Kansas City, Missouri
Kelly Kingman, Sticky eBooks, Beacon, New York
Tricia Lawrence, real/brilliant, inc.,
located near Seattle
Linda M. Lopeke (aka the SmartStart Coach),
Lexicorp Services Inc., Toronto, Ontario, Canada
Matt Mansfield, Matt About Business, LLC;
Deerfield, Illinois
Barbara Milgram, Pomegranate Planning,
Los Angeles, California
Kelly Newsome, Higher Ground Yoga, Washington, D.C.
Laura Petrolino, Ignite Venture Partners,
Tampa, Florida

Ted Prodromu, NetBizExpert, San Anselmo, California
Amy Pryor, Amy Pryor Fine Art,
Newport Beach, California
Cari Redondo, A Work of Heart By Cari, Marion, Iowa
Shannon Reece, Reece International LLC,
Naples, Florida
Angelique L. Rewers, The Corporate Agent™,
Baltimore, Maryland
Helen Robinett, Image Quest, Melbourne, Australia
Jill Salzman, The Founding Moms, Oak Park, Illinois
Jim Sheard, Ph.D., Beyond the Score,
Owatonna, Minnesota
Revka Stearns, Solopreneur Web Design, and Berries
and Cream Blog Design, Vanceboro, North Carolina
Natalia Sylvester, Inky Clean, Austin, Texas
Cindy Tonkin, The Consultants' Consultant,
Sydney, Australia
Caroline Colóm Vásquez, Paloma's Nest, Austin, Texas
Shayna Walker, Williamsburg Wedding Design,
Williamsburg, Virginia
Tommy Walker, Tommy.ismy.name,
Dover, New Hampshire

Chapter 1
Why Did You Start Your Business?

Nichole Bazemore: I wanted to see if I could do it successfully. I never enjoyed working in traditional corporate environments and wanted to do something which would indulge my creative passions and natural gifts and at the same time, allow me to design my work around my lifestyle rather than the other way around.

Amy Harrison: I had been working for a small group of private investors for a few years and got a huge buzz from the passion and the spirit they had for their businesses. I wanted that same spark of excitement for my own project so I branched out on my own.

Diana Guerrero: I had been working in a career with animals since the mid-1970s. I started the business after I began spending weekends in the mountains of Southern California. I was sick of the city and the ups and downs in the animal acting industry and the limited imagination in the more traditional animal-care facilities. The environment and location and way of life was attractive to me. So, I began searching for a business model that would work and started my animal business.

Barbara Milgram: I had worked in advertising and although I successfully climbed the corporate ladder, I began to grow more and more frustrated feeling that my opportunities to grow and contribute at my full potential were limited by the constraints of being part of a bigger organization. I wanted to try my hand at making a go of it on my own.

David Billings: Insanity runs in my family. Starting this business was just something I had to do. I had worked for studios and design firms for almost 10 years and I learned a ton. But I always felt that I had my own strange solutions and methods didn't always fit the mold. I decided that if I was ever going to do things the way I wanted, I would have to start my own company.

Andy Hayes: I was kind of forced. I had ended up after a series of corporate acquisitions inside of a company that I passionately disliked, working with people I disliked, doing work I disliked. I was depressed and had a lot of health issues because of it. I finally had had enough and said that even if I started a business and failed, I'd be better off. Thankfully, I was right. On the better-off part, not the fail part.

Bill Dwight: I grew up in Silicon Valley in a very entrepreneurial family. My dad founded a pioneering company in the laser industry in the early 1960s. So, I've always had this latent entrepreneurial gene, I've always loved to build stuff, and I've always admired the spirit and determination that entrepreneurs possess.

I have worked for five software startups over the years, but I never really got up the gumption to start my own thing from scratch.

Finally, almost five years ago, at age 43, I felt like the time was ,"now or never." At the same time, I had recently built something as a weekend project for my kids that I was realizing could have broad appeal and value. And, I loved the mission of helping parents become better mentors in preparing their kids for the real world. So, it was pretty much the perfect alignment of timing, my passions, and my skills as a (somewhat rusty) software developer.

Caroline Colóm Vásquez: I always had the entrepreneurial spirit in me, with the desire to create a tangible product from my art work. The online world allowed me to put my ideas in front of an international audience. By curating my own online shop, I am able to control how my products are presented and viewed. It also allows me the flexibility to be a mother, and, in the early days of the company, work from home when needed.

Heather Claus: I'm a rebel and a capitalist.

Kelly Kingman: I was looking for more independence and flexibility in my career and wanted a vehicle to help me leave my job, then I was laid off in a horrible economic downturn and going my own way seemed the only sensible option.

Laurie Gay: First, I wanted a career that met my

natural preferences for schedule and environment. For me, that means having a career that is location independent, meaning it permits me to live anywhere and still be earning a living. I also thrive when controlling my own schedule and creating a variety of work that suits my natural preferences and my strengths, like being around people, writing and speaking instead of, oh, I don't know, dying alone in an office. Second, I wanted a career that felt really fulfilling on a personal level. I believe I'm on the planet to change the world for the better, and I wanted my career to reflect my priorities.

Laura Brandenburg: At the time, I wanted to build my career in business analysis by accumulating diverse project experiences. I saw independent consulting as a means to broaden my perspective.

I am a driven individual and I was a bit jaded by seeing the investments I had made in my jobs help build significant monetary benefits for executives with whom I didn't always see eye-to-eye. I figured I owed it to myself to see if I could leverage that investment for a more direct personal benefit.

Cari Redondo: I originally was just making baby afghans for craft shows, and I had made myself some business cards with my computer and inkjet printer. I shared a business card with my hair stylist who said, "Hey, can you make me some business cards?" From there, the business evolved from a craft business to designing business cards and brochures for small businesses, professionals, and organizations.

When I left my "real job" because I couldn't deal with corporate culture and decisions, I had the opportunity to grow.

One January, I had two clients completely unrelated to each other tell two different friends to contact me about making their wedding invitations — even though I had never breathed the phrase "wedding invitations." Those two clients turned into a half dozen more clients, and I was officially in the wedding invitation business!

Deb Howard Greenleaf: To allow for a more flexible schedule and to explore my dream of being my own boss.

Also, the accounting firms that I'd worked in were staffed by generalists that would tackle almost anything accounting-related, but I wanted to focus on working with small-business owners.

Shayna Walker: I discovered around 2002 that I had developed a permanent disability that would prohibit me from working at a "normal" job (I had previously been a legal secretary) and from living where I was in Los Angeles. Not working wasn't an option financially or emotionally so I had to find a job that fit my altered lifestyle.

For various reasons, wedding planning was a great fit that let me use talents and skills I had already acquired while giving me the flexibility I needed to live with my new challenges.

Angelique Rewers: To eliminate external barriers (like a boss!) to achieving everything my heart desires. As a business owner, my success is limited only by my imagination.

Amy Pryor: The business was officially started because our family had experienced some difficult financial times due to the economy. I first started out teaching kids art from my daughter's second-grade class. Since my son was now going into kindergarten, I thought I had more time to explore selling my paintings. The classes started getting bigger and I needed to start offering more classes. I started having success selling my art, so I knew it was turning into more than a hobby.

Jim Sheard: I retired early at age 55 due to my bipolar disorder, and I needed something to occupy my mind and time. It has become a passion I pursue at home and at a local coffee shop I call my "office." Mine is more of an avocation than a business.

Bob Andelman: I have a stubborn independent streak. Not that I can't and don't play well with others, but I like to go at my own steady pace and make — and live with — my own decisions. I'm extremely self-motivated and ambitious in the sense that I know what I want to accomplish each day and day after day.

Chapter 2

What Was the Best Thing You Did When You Started Your Business?

Tzaddi Gordon: I subcontracted with a friend who already had a successful business. I learned a lot about business from working closely with her in my early years of freelancing. Her informal mentorship was immensely valuable and gave me a great jump-start on building a network.

David Billings: I had set aside enough to live on for about a year. I really needed more than that, but without even that cushion I would have had to throw in the towel very early. I would not be answering these questions right now, that's for sure.

Linda Lopeke: Every contract was set up in a way that gave me absolute creative control and ownership of the intellectual property created. And, after one of the early clients defaulted on a critical deal leaving me financially stranded, I amended our standard contract so that I was always paid in advance. That ended all worrying about cash flow. Our corporate lawyer thought I was insane. But it's really all in how you position these things with clients. That's the really great thing about being a solopreneur — you get to conduct business exactly how you want to because you are in charge!

Heather Claus: I did what felt right to me. In 1996 NO ONE thought online sewing classes would work. I proved them very wrong.

Bob Andelman: I was willing to do anything related to writing to survive. Instead of pursuing unrelated jobs, I wrote anything I could to gain experience and make new contacts: articles, of course, but also press releases, speeches, corporate reports, brochures, you name it.

Caroline Colóm Vásquez: Moving my studio and office operations out of my home. As an entrepreneur it has always been difficult to separate home and work life; to have the physical separation between home and work has helped create some balance in an otherwise hectic schedule and lifestyle.

Cari Redondo: I did not go into debt, and kept my overhead low — I never had to worry about hitting a minimum, so I was very focused on giving customers what they needed with a lot of personal attention.

Barbara Milgram: Despite the conventional wisdom and advice of many people, I actually did not have a master plan and this turned out to be more helpful than I would have thought.

Without something etched in stone, I was able to remain flexible so I could evolve and adjust to new realities, aligning my talent and interests with the marketplace as it did its own zigs and zags.

Bill Dwight: I think one of the best things I did was open up the initial unpolished application to a group of "charter" families very early on, but simultaneously resist the prevailing "common wisdom" of throwing it out there too early to the general public.

I think it was the right compromise: I wanted to get a lot of hands-on feedback to steer us in the right direction, but I also wanted to launch with something we could be really, really proud of. I hate visiting a "launched" site and getting the feeling that it's hacked together quickly, or, worse, that I'm doing their quality assurance for them.

We made sure our charter family members knew that they were guinea pigs and that they were O.K. with helping us refine the service prior to launch.

Jill Salzman: Oddly enough, the best thing I did was to pick a company name that was vague and allowed me to grow. If I had called it Paperwork Management, doing booking and publicity for clients would not have been as successful. But with Paperwork Media there was much room for growth, and I did grow into different areas.

Kelly Kingman: I joined a few forums of other new or would-be entrepreneurs—they've provided a sounding board for my ideas, a wellspring of support, a great professional network and some of my first clients.

Matt Mansfield: I hired a marketing/product-development person to help. Not only is she a great sounding board, idea generator and advisor, but she also acts as a coach, assuring I stay on track and put dates next to each to-do.

Laura Petrolino: Realize that "it takes a village." No man is an island, and that is especially true for business owners. I reached out to those around me and offered to help them with their businesses in any way I could.

I worked to form coalitions with fellow business owners, create a referral train and donate my services in little ways when I could. This type of partnering and relationship building is a core component of all of the campaigns I develop for my clients, thus a core component of my own business planning and outreach.

Laurie Gay: I hired several different people to help me get clear on exactly how I was going to make this thing work, and exactly what I wanted it to look like. You need support, and if your resources are limited, there are a lot of very good, free options, too, for marketing yourself and creating a foundation for your business that will grow with you.

Sherice Jacob: I spent every waking moment learning everything I could about Web design and writing. I studied countless courses, books, and then put everything I knew into practice. I still read a considerable amount to this day. You HAVE to in this kind of business. You can't afford to fall behind.

Tricia Lawrence: The best thing I did was to stay small for as long as I could. I worked for almost seven years out of an 8 x 8-foot closet and somehow that physical barrier kept me small.

It was a real mindset change to move to a bigger office and I immediately got into trouble and overbooked myself, bought unnecessary technology and equipment, and lost track of my personal goals.

Amy Harrison: Turn my life upside down to support my work. We were living in a two-bedroom flat, one bedroom was used to take language students to help with the bills and the other bedroom was converted into an office space. We even got rid of the bed and slept on a foam mattress. It wasn't stressful, though; it was good fun and exciting!

Deb Howard Greenleaf: I started my business very slowly, taking on only a few new clients at a time. This allowed me to work on my systems, learn how quickly I could turn around a given type of project, and learn where my niche was.

It only took a year for me to realize that my target clients were other solo professionals who wanted someone else to bear the burden of invoicing, collections, and balancing the books.

Amy Pryor: I think the best thing so far has been getting involved in social media.

So far, all of my sales and my art classes are from my personal network. That can only go so far to sustain or grow a business. I started a Facebook page, than added a Twitter account, and about three weeks ago I started blogging. Spending time with those media has allowed me to interact with people I would never had met otherwise.

Marianne Cantwell: Wrote my blog, and put it out

there fast — without worrying about whether it was good enough or whether I had "permission" to say what I was saying.

My writing got me to where I am — for example, within 3 months of starting I was quoted as an expert in a book, simply because the author came across my blog. My approach and voice and ultimately, my whole business, came out of writing.

The saddest thing I see is when I hear people say "I have a blog but I'm not ready to share it with the world yet" — only when you do share it with the world will you figure out how to make it as fabulous as you imagine!

Natalia Sylvester: I relaunched as Inky Clean [copywriting and editing firm] because I wanted to build a brand that was memorable to the people I most wanted to work with. Prior to that, my company was just my name and the title "Freelance Writer," which didn't convey much about what I do or how I do it.

I realized that if I was going to focus on helping startups and small businesses build their brand and show some personality, I had to lead by example. It's made all the difference — I've built longer relationships with more clients, and more importantly, they're the clients that are right for me.

Jim Sheard: I coauthored with people who had insights beyond my own.

Nichole Bazemore: I took four months off to read, research, sleep in, go to my son's baseball games, and spend time at the beach. I cleared my mind of everything everyone said I was "supposed" to do and gave myself time to dream about and plan for what I wanted to do.

Patrick Curtis: I made sure that I focused on a niche I knew well AND I made sure that it was fun. That niche was investment banking and the fun was making monkeys the overarching theme of the community (it's what people in the industry call the junior analysts). Sometimes being a little quirky and bringing some "flavor" to a serious industry makes you more memorable.

Burton Kelso: I took the time to think about the type of equipment I would need for my business before I purchased it.

Every day I see many businesses (big and small)

purchase equipment without thinking about the long-term aspects of those purchases. It's a waste of time and money when you are replacing equipment every 18 months.

With the exception of my computers, the equipment I purchased for my business lasted many months after my first 10 years of business. I also took the time to think about my business model and what day-to-day processes I wanted to put into place. I still use those processes today.

Chapter 3
What Is a Mistake You Made That You Have Learned From?

David Billings: Trying to appeal to everyone. When I first started, I was so anxious about getting clients and bringing in revenue that I started trying to fit into every opportunity that came up. "You need a corporate-looking brochure? Well, I don't really do those, but maybe I could adapt myself to."

Things got really messy, scattered, and depressing. I didn't know who I was anymore, or who I was trying to please. Hmm. Everyone? That's pretty tough to do.

It's also ironic, because it's the same reason I struck out on my own — to do my own thing.

Amy Harrison: Discounting too much and not taking a deposit. In the early days it was just great to get work so you're prepared to slash your prices. This just leads to burnout though and you send the wrong message to clients, you're telling them that your words are cheap.

Burton Kelso: During my first years of business, I did not do a good job of keeping in contact with my customers. I assumed that after one service visit, they would be lifelong customers. As a result, I lost a lot of customers.

You have to stay in constant contact with your customer base. There is no customer loyalty unless you create it. It's important to let your customers know how important they are to you. Calling with birthday wishes, random acts of communication and customer appreciation events are a must if you want to stay in business and grow your business.

Nichole Bazemore: For the first 10 months or so, I compared myself to every copywriter in the world. That's a recipe for disaster. I downplayed my gifts, told myself I wasn't good enough, and counted myself out. I've since learned to appreciate my gifts and focus my time on being the very best me that I can be.

Helen Robinett: You need to be better at marketing than doing.

Jim Sheard: I failed to get started exercising and eating properly until just recently. It led to some health-risk factors.

Linda Lopeke: The biggest mistake I made in the early years was believing the buying decision is made on price. (It isn't. It's made on emotion and justified with logic later.)

Another huge mistake I made (and I've made it three times now — once for each decade I've been in business) was ignoring my gut instinct in favour of trusting people who proved themselves unworthy of my trust. (Lesson learned: When people show you who they really are, you need to believe them, the first time!)

Revka Stearns: I have made too many mistakes to count and have learned from many of them. One of the biggest lessons I've learned has been to filter potential clients, not taking every project that comes my way. The stress and headaches involved in working with clients and on projects that aren't a good fit for me are not worth any amount of money I might make.

Barbara Milgram: It's a mistake to give clients exactly what they ask for just to keep them happy (unless you think it will solve their problem).

In the end, what makes a client happy is getting breakthrough learning — and achieving this means sometimes adjusting plans a bit. Clients are happiest when they get more than they imagined was possible and pulling this off can mean pushing beyond a comfort zone to find the golden nugget that lives way outside the box.

Bill Dwight: I waited too long to find a great outside graphic/Web designer. I know great design when I see it, but I sure don't know how to produce it myself (you should have seen the first versions of the FamZoo UI that I designed — yech!).

Design is a real craft. It also takes quite a bit of time and attention to detail to implement the design once you have it. So, I probably set us back by a good 6-12 months by waiting too long.

Caroline Colóm Vásquez: Not getting help soon enough. When I first started my business, many months were extremely overwhelming; we experienced a big demand for our product very early on. As exciting as this was, it was also difficult on myself and my family.

Had I only learned to delegate tasks that others could do, much of this stress may have been avoided.

Kelly Kingman: I waited a very long time before creating my first product. I've learned that the sooner you create something, the sooner you can test it in the marketplace. Now that I launched one eBook, I can't wait to do more — not just because of the income, but the creative rush of solving problems and helping people get their eBooks written.

Koldo Barroso: To resist accepting who I am.

Laura Petrolino: Sadly, being too trusting. I prefer to do things with "a handshake," but I soon learned that that was the quickest way to be taken advantage of. This is sad to me, because I prefer to work with clients as friends. I hold up my side of the agreement, you hold up yours. I like working in a environment of complete trust. Unfortunately, I learned I had to protect myself, so now I have stricter contracts and payment terms.

Laurie Gay: Don't take on too much too quickly. I tried to start several avenues of my business all at once, while moving cities and traveling for fun. It was way too much, and I got very little done until I shaved off some less-necessary commitments.

Shayna Walker: I accrued personal debt to finance my business during a time when my personal life (i.e. my former marriage) was very unstable. It magnified an already bad situation and contributed to years of financial instability which I still see traces of now. I learned a lot from those early mistakes.

Tricia Lawrence: The mistake was growing too fast and going into debt as a business. Worst decision hands down. While there is a place for limited debt load for small businesses, the best and most stable small businesses who are growing pledge to be rid of the debt as quickly as possible (or to keep a handle on it so that it's manageable).

Small businesses are under more pressure than ever and especially over the past few years, those with hefty business loans or those who take way too big risks are really struggling.

Tommy Walker: Working without a contract is something that I will not ever do again. That and giving a strategy in a proposal. Too often with people in this industry, one person's proposal is another person's shopping list to find goods at a lower cost. Instead I choose to explain my methodology in a way that a potential client can see working for them.

Dawn Svenson Holland: I dropped the ball on key timing with a prospective client due to a family emergency and offered the client free services to accept responsibility for my error. Yes, "giving away my value" violates everything my SCORE consultant shared. But I was in the wrong and needed to be accountable for my error. I was reminded through this experience that accountability is a fundamental footing in building any business.

Deb Howard Greenleaf: My biggest mistakes have all involved over-promising—agreeing to a deadline before I knew the true extent of the work to be done. After working round-the-clock to meet those deadlines, I learned to ask a lot more questions upfront and always build in a very wide margin to my deadlines.

Heather Claus: I structured my first business so that no matter how successful it was, it could not grow beyond my own capabilities or without me.

Shannon Reece: I got caught up in a cycle of perfectionism when I first started out. I could have easily created a simple blog and worked on building an email list, while other work was being completed behind the scenes. Instead, I waited until every last detail was finished, and lost a lot of valuable time in the process. Fear can really get in the way of progress if you let it call the shots.

Bob Andelman: I had to learn early on to temper the expression of my opinions and my sense of humor. Whatever I believe personally (or find amusing) doesn't mean the person hiring me shares those beliefs. What matters is completing a job, on time, being pleasant and agreeable to the people or company paying my fee.

Laura Brandenburg: Early in my blogging career I assumed I had to answer every e-mail and respond to every question individually. As my blog and readership grew, this became impossible to sustain.

I've learned that I can still be personal and responsive using some automation and support tools. I've had to shift my focus to enable my blog to grow. While I still listen carefully and craft content to meet the needs of my readers, not every e-mail is individually written. I learned to balance responsiveness with sustainability.

Ted Prodromu: My business was project-based, with little recurring revenue.

Angelique Rewers: I spent a lot of time and money doing something that wasn't working — and by not working I mean it was costing me money versus bringing in money — but that I kept doing because I wasn't willing to admit it was a failure.

Amy Pryor: It's a toss-up between two things.

One is not have a good handle on how to run a business. Things like good bookkeeping, necessary licenses, paying taxes etc. I even wrote a blog about it titled, "Wow, Starting a Business is REALLY Tough."

The second thing is regarding attracting fans. I thought if I keep putting stuff out there, people will become a fan on Facebook or follow me on Twitter. The more I read about social media and search engine optimization, the more I realized I was going about it backwards. I need to write content that allows people who are searching for fine art to find me. Luckily I hadn't been doing it very long and I didn't need to back track or anything. I just needed to adjust from that point on.

Patrick Curtis: I underestimated the importance of site performance and took too long getting the site on a more powerful server and themed properly.

As soon as the site performance improved, traffic jumped and we've never looked back.

Tzaddi Gordon: Not making enough time to work ON the business and to relax. I've always put my clients first and I've come to realize that if you neglect the needs of your business or yourself then it's a disservice to the clients in the long run. It's another thing I'm still working on.

Jill Salzman: Which one? From this week or the last several weeks? Every day brings a new bump in the road. And I learn from every single one (don't you?).

Chapter 4
What Lifestyle Changes Have You Made To Stay In Business?

Caroline Colóm Vásquez: Being your own boss is the most difficult job you will ever have. There seems to never be a time or day when you are not working in some way, shape, or form. Sacrifices are made when it comes to social life, schedule, and priorities. It is a choice and a commitment, but it can also be the most gratifying way to live. In many ways, you control your own destiny.

Amy Harrison: Cutting back on spending, and spending more time with positive people. When you have a job, a moan at the watercooler is a bit of a bonding exercise, but when you're trying to get your business off the ground there's just no space for that kind of mentality. You've got to believe you can do it and look for people who will support that and encourage you.

David Billings: As a family, we've had to significantly lower our standard of living. In my last job I was making six figures. Keeping the business going sometimes means living in less-than-sexy digs and driving one used car.

Tzaddi Gordon: The form of my business and my lifestyle choices go hand in hand. I wanted to move out of the city. Working from home in a rural area means my daily expenses are lower than they were in a city life of commuting and working in a big corporation. Therefore it's O.K. to earn less than I used to. I'm sure I could earn a lot more if I wanted to do business differently, but I care more about the kind of work I'm doing and my values than I do the money.

Sherice Jacob: Health insurance is a royal pain for solo business owners. Especially if you live in a state like West Virginia and every company just assumes you're a health risk because of where your STATE ranks on some kind of health and wellness scale.

Angelique Rewers: The biggest decision has been to hire a nanny for our twins versus becoming a stay-at-home mom. I know there are things I miss out on during the day when I'm working. But I feel more fulfilled being a mom and a business owner, and I think I'm better in both roles because of what I learn from the other.

Kelly Newsome: I live very simply and started saving a couple of years before starting my business (I didn't know what I was saving for, just "something else.") I work at home (and coffee shops) to eliminate office-space rent. I make sure to meet friends for drinks during happy hour specials. I shop less, travel less. But I live more.

Shayna Walker: The biggest lifestyle choices have been to forego medical care for myself (my children are covered by their father) and the sacrifice of a lot of time over the years, especially the early ones; it's time that I could have spent exclusively with my kids.

Being a solopreneur has been as much a benefit as

a sacrifice on that front, though. I have the flexibility now to be a part of my children's education and daily life that I wouldn't if I were stuck in an office job.

Also, my kids are being raised in a culture of entrepreneurism that has already given them confidence and a free spirit unlike other kids their age.

I also drive an old, kind of decaying vehicle, rarely take vacations and I live in an apartment instead of a house. I hope that I'm on the path to financial freedom at some point, but in the meantime, I sacrifice a lot of the "shiny" things for a freedom of a different kind.

Revka Stearns: I home-schooled my three girls for three years. I found out I can't be a full-time mom/wife/homemaker, teacher, and solopreneur. Everything, particularly the girls' education, was suffering.

So this year they're in school — and loving it.

Sometimes I feel like putting them in school says I didn't love them as much as I love my business, but I know that the truth of the matter is that I hated teaching and that is why I did such a bad job of it. My business just provided me an easy way to escape doing what I didn't want to do in the first place.

Chapter 5
What Are Your Strategies For Staying Competitive?

Andy Hayes: There's a flaw in that old chestnut, "Keep your Friends Close and Your Enemies Closer." Often if you spend too much time obsessing on competitors, you forget about innovation. So there's a balance there.

For me, I find innovation when I'm away from my world. I read classic literature and study Buddhist meditation. I see what's hot, what's changing, and what I can use from other industries. The ideas will come.

Marianne Cantwell: Know your people and focus on them, not on what other businesses are going. Don't read what others are doing in your field. If you avidly read every newsletter of your "comparables" (I prefer that term to "competitors") then you'll end up unconsciously imitating what they do and you'll end up with a shadow of their original.

Mel DePaoli: Closely aligning myself to people who you would initially think are my competition. They make great referral sources and allow me to focus on projects I want to work on.

Angelique Rewers: When it comes to distinguishing yourself from the competition, there's no substitute for being the best in your industry. So I'm always striving to expand my knowledge and expertise, hone my marketing skills and enhance my client service.

Amy Harrison: Taking on less work. I look for a long-term relationship with my clients, even if it's only a short-term project. I want to give them as much of my time as possible when we work together so I can nurture that relationship and show them that I really care about their business.

That's quite an investment on my part and I can only do it by not overworking.

Natalia Sylvester: Aside from actively marketing myself and networking both online and in person, my biggest focus is on building my brand and making sure it stays consistent throughout a customer's experience.

David Billings: My only strategy is being completely unique. That way I don't have to compete.

Helen Robinett: Niche value. No one approaches this work the way I do. I tend to break the rules. People like that.

Revka Stearns: I'm always looking for opportunities to learn new things. I love looking at my friends who are also my competitors to see what direction they're taking. I often get new ideas from seeing what they are doing. Reading articles and magazines relating to my field of work also keeps me updated on industry changes and trends.

Dawn Svenson Holland: Deliver service that reflects the deep and abiding respect I have for the amazing work nonprofit staff and volunteers do. Respond to all e-mails and voicemails within 24 hours. Keep the focus on what the client needs instead of how much business I close in any given month. Take the time to understand client needs up front and offer project quotes accordingly.

Deb Howard Greenleaf: Provide awesome customer service, as this will differentiate you from the pack. To date, most of my business has come from referrals from happy clients. I still stink at self-promotion, so referral marketing is my cup of tea!

Diana Guerrero: Being creative, progressive, and helpful are the big three. I think offering good-quality service is essential, along with ease of access and a solid track record.

Really, I think the customer-service piece is becoming even more critical. People want to connect in an authentic manner and so if you do, you'll come out ahead.

Another investment I make is that I am an avid continuing education person. Although I've always taught courses, I make sure that I am enrolled in multiple online programs and networking groups where

I can keep up with the changes in my industry and business in general.

Nichole Bazemore: I read, study, and try to avoid social networking and the Internet at least one day a week. It helps me to re-center.

Koldo Barroso: To be myself. We're all one-of-a-kind in this world. If life has been generous enough to give us the opportunity to experience ourselves the way we are, then there must be a way that we can make other people happy giving the best that we have, which is our uniqueness.

I don't compete with other artists and I don't give a damn if they're better or worse than I am. I only compete with myself and each day I try to be more authentic so my spirit reaches my audience in the most faithful and honest way. Which is not easy at all, but it is exciting.

Laurie Gay: I actually don't view today's environment as one of competition in a traditional sense. I maintain my client base and keep clients best when I am living by my own advice and partnering with and sharing clients and information openly with would-be competitors.

I find that growing really clear on who you are serving, and what keeps that specific person up at night and then solving their juiciest problems for them is the best way to create a viable business.

I don't try to beat or outdo other people doing similar work as I do, but riff off of their ideas as they do mine. It's really fun, and it's a model that's working very well.

Shayna Walker: I pursue as many educational opportunities as I can possibly afford each year.

My greatest pleasure is attending conferences (I keep trying to figure out how to do that as a career), meeting people in my industry from every corner of the world and exchanging ideas.

I also view competitors as colleagues, which has opened up whole new worlds of opportunity.

Tommy Walker: I let the work speak for itself. My rates are pretty competitive compared to the rest of the industry, but on one client I'm able to live comfortably. I let word of mouth and quality of work do its thing mostly.

I'm not really interested in throwing down the gauntlet with competitors, because there are plenty who know far more than I do, and likewise those who aren't quite where I'm at now in terms of knowledge. So I learn from who I can, and educate who I can as well.

Tricia Lawrence: My strategies for staying competitive are to never settle. I never rest on my laurels. I keep pushing.

I get bored frequently, so I need something new more often than not. I'm also an overachiever, so I have to outsmart myself sometimes (being born on the same day as Martha Stewart, the queen of Type A overachievement, is the only reason I can think of for this).

Amy Pryor: That is such a good question. You probably know there is an ocean full of artists. I have found that most artists do not like the marketing or selling aspect. I feel like my business skills will give me a great advantage because I'll do a lot more things to get my art in front of people. Unfortunately, most artists want to wait for a prospect to find them.

I also think artists make mistakes about pricing their art. I'm just starting out, so I think my prices are very reasonable for an emerging artist. Also, the economy is tough. Home prices have come down, interest rates are lower and stock prices are down. Why should it be a negative to think art prices should come down as well?

I think embracing social media and learning SEO will be a strong advantage.

Jim Sheard: I do not compete. I just try to be the best "me" possible.

Chapter 6

What Is Your Biggest Current Challenge and What Are You Doing to Solve It?

Barbara Milgram: Staying creative and innovative given shrinking budgets and timelines. Clients feel pressure to do more with less, especially over the past year, and the burden falls squarely on my shoulders to provide fresh, original thinking despite time and cost constraints.

I need to always remain open and curious and push myself to figure out new ways of designing research so that originality or creativity are never compromised, even when timelines and resources are.

As a solopreneur, it's also a challenge to fill the pipeline for new business while juggling the demands of current projects. I continually struggle with this —

there's just so much time in the day. That said, I'm committing more time each week to marketing and filling the pipeline than I have in the past and trying to look at this effort as productive and useful rather than a distraction from current client work.

Linda Lopeke: Distraction is the #1 enemy of success. With so much happening in the digital world, I have to constantly remind myself to ignore the lure of bright, shiny objects (just call me "gadget girl") and concentrate on the priorities at hand. (Technology is great but some days nothing beats a sharp pencil and a blank sheet of paper.)

Cari Redondo: My biggest business challenge is how to keep improving the value that I provide to my clients within the structure of my business.

David Billings: Right now my challenge is growing out of a service business into a solutions business. I love working with my clients, but I need to develop products and services that don't require my direct attention.

For example, there are people who want to work

with me one-on-one but can't afford it. I still want to help them, but I also can't afford to work for free or lower my rates. So I'm creating some products that will get them the help they need at a rate they can afford.

This way I can also focus my energy on a few choice clients every month, rather than packing my schedule to make sure I have revenue coming in.

Helen Robinett: Social media marketing. I am about to engage a guru to help with it. Definitely not my skill set.

Burton Kelso: Our current business market is over-saturated with Solo-Geeks and Mass Market Geeks who are all making the same promises of solving computer and technology issues cheaper and faster.

My solution has been to be a technology professional who cares about people and my community. I donate services and products to local non-profit and needy organizations on a regular basis. It's important to be an individual who has a general interest in helping our environment and community.

I've also embraced social media as in many in my

industry have not. Social media helps me keep in contact with my current customer base while exposing my business to a personal and professional community that I would not normally encounter in my day-to-day interactions.

Kelly Kingman: Managing overwhelm. I am managing it by taking one day at a time and doing what I can to renew my energy when it's time to unplug — meaning shutting down my computer at the end of the work day and trying not to check my e-mail every 5 minutes on my phone.

Koldo Barroso: Without a doubt, breaking out my career in a new country and in a moment when the publishing industry is about to re-invent itself. Today, new authors and illustrators like me are not precisely welcomed by AR's and agents regardless of our talent and potential to reach a wide audience. This seems to be the worst moment in history to start a career as an author, but I see it as a wonderful possibility to take part of a beautiful change in the scheme of things.

There's a lot of things that can be better in the future of the publishing world, and this is the time.

Thanks to the Internet, we authors and artists have the possibility of connecting with our potential audience without the interference of middle people. We can establish a more human relationship with our audience and have more control over our product at the same time.

Nichole Bazemore: Collecting late invoices. I hate playing bill collector. It literally turns my stomach. Luckily, I have a great bookkeeper who has taken on this task for me!

Laurie Gay: Currently, my biggest challenge is creating systems that work for my idiosyncratic business so that everything is streamlined (keeping books, creating files for clients, building new offerings). Time is an issue, and systems really are the answer for saving time for the solopreneur.

That said, we all do such unique ventures that your systems don't always look like the next guy's, so you have to see what shape your business takes and continue to modify your systems accordingly as your very alive business grows and changes with you.

Matt Mansfield: I believe my biggest challenge, and one likely faced by all solopreneurs, is the fact that I have to do it all. I built and manage the Web site. I write content and I handle all the back-office details (the books, legal, etc.).

I am working to put both people and systems in place, not employees but other business folks who can share the burden for a fee. Of course, I need to earn before that happens.

Shayna Walker: Cash flow for projects beyond the scope of the day-to-day business is my biggest challenge. I have some great specialty things in the works, but it's always tough to fund the new stuff. Bootstrapping has its appeal and is full of learning experiences, though.

Sherice Jacob: Finding more time for projects that grow my business. I am working toward setting aside a couple of hours a day just for my own projects — I'm hoping it will become a permanent habit!

Tommy Walker: My biggest challenge in this business is dealing with people's hurt from working with snake-oil companies that took their money and ran. Instead of talking about how awesome I am, I let my work speak for itself, and let my clients do the referring for me. That way I'm not pounding on anyone's door for work, and they're already getting an active example of the work I do on a regular basis.

Tricia Lawrence: My biggest current challenge in my business is shifting gears from one service offering to another. I am trying to quit doing work that I've been doing for 15 years and that turns my soul into a gaping void.

I am attempting to take on more work that I truly love. I'm trying to let my creativity run free and to have more allowance. The way I'm doing this is to bootstrap (no debt) even when I actually need something and to cut back on the seemingly limitless amounts of dribbling work that bores me and to pursue (even though it doesn't seem like I find enough of it) the work I want to do.

Bob Andelman: As a writer, traditional avenues such as magazine and newspaper writing have dried up and book publishing is going through titanic shifts.

Just as I did when I started out, I'm prepared to take on non-traditional assignments and apply my writing skills and creativity in new arenas.

On the radio side, the content isn't the issue; making the show's voice heard in a sea of noise is. Word-of-mouth has been replaced by word-of-tweet.

Amy Pryor: I think my biggest challenge now is finding more people interested in buying fine art. Luxury items are items that people stop buying when the economy is poor. They may be remodeling a house, but their budget is being cut, so they might be looking for prints instead of originals.

Some of things I am doing to solve it is keep my prices reasonable, offer digital prints and volume discounts. Social media is definitely another way I am trying to overcome this challenge.

Laura Brandenburg: Right now I am learning how to effectively market both my products and other high-value products to my community. While marketing my products has come naturally to me, converting on third-party products has proved more of a challenge and something I want to overcome. There is so much great work out there in our profession and I want to help my audience find the best possible products to advance their careers.

A second challenge for me is around building a scalable mentoring practice. My vision is to help individuals with their careers, and while I find this rewarding, the sales and fulfillment process can be quite consuming. I'm currently experimenting with different business models, practices, and processes to find the right approach for my business.

Deb Howard Greenleaf: I am still trying to find the sweet spot where I'm hitting my monthly profit goals but not working extra hours after the kids are in bed. I think I'm like a lot of soloists who face months that are either feast or famine, tons of work or not enough.

To meet this challenge, I've been refining my systems to plan ahead, anticipate busy periods and shift some of my routine work to other weeks where the workload isn't so heavy.

Chapter 7
Where Do You Want To Be With the Business In Five Years?

Matt Mansfield: I want to continue growing the site offerings and sense of community. There's an opportunity to create a great spot online here, one where folks share and learn best practices in a low-key, nonintimidating way and I'm going to work hard to make that a reality. I'd like to expand my role beyond the site as well through both speaking and writing.

Melissa Dinwiddie: In five years I'd love to have a loyal community of 500+ paid subscribers, and a readership/fan base of many times that. I'd like to be creating new content that excites me (including getting back to making visual art) and makes a positive difference for my customers. I'd like to have a true business that I can leave for a month or two at a time, knowing it will run just fine without me, as opposed to a job that requires my presence to make anything happen!

I'd also love to have a published book, and to be speaking and teaching workshops around the world.

Most of all, I'd like to be spending the vast majority of my time doing the things I'm most passionate about—creating content, creating art, creating music, creating connections, making a difference. AND I'd like to have plenty of "chill time" to boot!

Andy Hayes: I have no idea. Ask me again in 4.

Caroline Colóm Vásquez: I plan to expand the Paloma's Nest product line to include additional home furnishings and home accessories for all occasions and all rooms of the house. We will be expanding our wholesale division and attending the major gift and handcraft shows across the country. We see this as a key to building our brand recognition.

Tricia Lawrence: I want to stay bootstrapped for the next five years and to build new pieces of this business that I can't even yet fathom. That's very exciting to me in this season of massive change in publishing and marketing. I want to be wildly creative and not be inhibited by the economy. I want to not worry about where the money will come from next month so that I can focus on how I feel and what I want to do each morning. It sounds like a pipe dream, but I've made decisions toward this: we cut cable and got Netflix, we cut going out to eat, the latte factor, and overseas vacations in exchange for local road trips. I don't sign up for as many information products that I used to purchase. I have a list of what I already have and I just get an idea and then go search through my piles of already purchased infoproducts to find what I can use to make it happen.

Dawn Svenson Holland: Exceeding the income of the position I left for this new venture.

Sherice Jacob: I'd like to make it so that much of the routine work is more automated or managed without my direct intervention or supervision. I'd love to hire a virtual assistant or two in a couple of years (that is, if I can stand to relinquish control of some of the everyday stuff!).

Kelly Newsome: In five years, I expect my private client base to be limited to a small, carefully-selected number, allowing me to spend the rest of my time doing something. Something awesome. It's about all I know right now, and I'm O.K. with that.

Amy Harrison: I'd love to be in a position where I can hire other copywriters to grow the business, as well as running affordable copywriting courses.

Amy Pryor: I think the best way to answer that is to compare it with another artist who is about seven years into her career. That's Chandra Michaels of Sugarluxe.com. She has a thriving digital art business. She did it all herself and she is incredibly knowledgeable about social media. She has a team of employees and interns and, of course, has a profitable business. I hope five years from now, someone is describing me in that way. I would also like people from around the world to see a painting of mine and say, "that looks like an Amy Pryor."

Jim Sheard: I want to be well-known and appreciated for the things I have written and the products I have developed. I want "beyond the score" to be understood as a lifestyle in which relationships are more important than winning or losing; my logo to be recognizable to a large segment of the population, especially golfers. I want my colleagues, family, friends, and readers to feel they have benefited from what I have shared with them.

Kelly Kingman: In five years I would like to branch out into being an eBook publisher, making Sticky eBooks an imprint, like ChangeThis.com—finding great authors to help package and promote their work.

David Billings: South France. I'm only half kidding.

The thing is, I have a lifestyle business. Meaning, as long as I make the income I need and stay profitable, I don't need to scale it into a large firm with 30 employees.

In five years I would love to be busy enough to hire a couple employees and maintain a small office. I'm kind of an anomaly in the art world because I love the business side. I love marketing and meeting with people, so it would be nice to do more of that and have designers working on production. It would also be fun to develop junior designers and help them eventually start their own businesses.

Angelique Rewers: Five years from now I see my business being a true change agent in the small-business world.

Laura Brandenburg: If I could answer the question, "what will you be doing this time next year?", I'd consider myself an insightful person! Truth be told, this journey has continued to surprise me at every turn. While I don't know the specifics, I do know that this time next year I'll be helping business analysts on their career journeys. I want to be in a position where I can live solely from my income helping business analysts so I can pick and choose my project work. In five years, I imagine I'll be continuing to build on this mission but I can't pretend to know what life has in store for me over that long of a time frame.

Deb Howard Greenleaf: Still in business, doing what I love!

Chapter 8
What Is Your Fallback Plan?

Tricia Lawrence: If my business should fail? I would immediately start another business. I often wonder what I would be if I didn't do this business and nothing ever interests me. I feel that I can be whatever I want as a solopreneur and can't bear the thought of signing myself up for a full-time career working for someone else.

Nichole Bazemore: It won't fail. If the commercial copywriting industry took a dive or I burnt out on the work, I would readjust and write family histories, documentaries, screenplays — even Twitter updates, if I had to! As long as humans have a need to communicate, there will always be a market for someone to tell their stories.

Amy Harrison: I don't have one because I can't really focus on making this work if there's an alternative in the back of my head. But, if things changed, I'd figure it out then.

Sherice Jacob: I have a bachelor's degree in Spanish education and a master's in media studies so I can put either of those to use.

Marianne Cantwell: My model is to start out small with no investment and innovate in fast iterations (in other words: do things, put 'em out there and tweak as you go). I know that, now, I can start something else in almost any field and make it work should I choose to. To me, knowing that you have everything you need right inside your head, to always ensure you have a good income…well, that is real freedom.

Laurie Gay: Well, two things: first, I don't believe in failure. Seriously. It's just reformulating and trying something different. Second, there isn't "a" fallback position; there are about a million fallback positions! I could find another coaching niche like, look for counseling positions at law schools (because of my legal background), return full-time to the practice of law or any number of other jobs.

My personal experience has been that there are a lot of jobs and opportunities out there — maybe just not ones that we are used to seeing.

There's a terrific Chinese saying, "Fishing is best when waters are choppy." There are some of the best opportunities in distressed markets that we wily solopreneurs are scooping up left, right and center. Join in on the fun.

Jill Salzman: Failure is not an option. If I make it so, it becomes a possibility and I refuse to make fear-based choices.

Cindy Tonkin: My business failing is not even an option.

Amy Pryor: I can't think that way.

Diana Guerrero: *sigh* I've had two setbacks — the first was a fall that rendered me disabled for a while and without an income and ability to produce—and that is how I got into the writing.

The second hurdle was my recent health issues; fortunately I had some investment accounts but long-term health stuff wiped me out and I am starting over — which is why I am working on the online business models — to avoid the vulnerability.

Dawn Svenson Holland: Find a nonprofit or community-minded organization I believe in and help them move missions forward.

Kelly Newsome: Legal consulting is an option; I'd look in the nonprofit sphere ideally, because I love service work. If that doesn't fly, though, I'd figure it out. If you work hard, act professionally, write well, and stay open to opportunity, someone'll usually hire you, and there are lots of options if you're open. Bartending. Nannying. Retail. Pizza delivery. I'm a hustler.

David Billings: I don't have a fallback. I used to rely on the fact that my old company would hire me back, but I've since let that go. My business won't fail. That sounds arrogant or overconfident. What I mean is that it might falter a bit and I may need to regroup while working for someone else. Even if I had to do that, it would be with an eye toward keeping the business going, or regenerating.

Helen Robinett: Start another business!

Patrick Curtis: I could always go back into finance (private equity or investment banking), but more likely I would join a startup because I love the thought of being part of a small team and outworking the competition.

Tzaddi Gordon: I don't have a fall-back position. The only failure I can imagine is if I failed to evolve the business. Businesses are living things that must adapt over time, just like Web sites. It's a good thing I'm wired for learning and challenges!

Koldo Barroso: To me, success means learning to fail. So if I fail again, I will always be me and pull myself together and keep going on. All things pass in this life: failure, success.

I don't believe in money as a measurement of success. Money is an energy that can move many things but it depends on us if this will make us and other people happy. To me, the only one that really pays at the end of the day is love and the one that really doesn't, is fear.

Shannon Reece: I am on a "no option to fail" mission, so there is no plan B. That is how I think solopreneurs need to approach their business — with 100% commitment. If you are not all in, how could you possibly expect to succeed?

Chapter 9
What Is Your Advice For Aspiring Solopreneurs?

Shannon Reece: Really make sure that you are pursuing a business option that taps into your greatest strengths, and is not an area where you will be daily working to overcome your weaknesses.

As a solopreneur, you will have to do it all for a while, and that will include tasks that are more difficult for you, or are not a part of your repertoire. Regardless, the core of your business should be designed around who you are, your values, interests and strengths, as well as, be a direction that will meet your income needs.

Starting your own business can be a long, rough road, but when you are doing what you love, it is worth the effort.

David Billings: Show up. Seriously. Nothing happens overnight, so you have to keep showing up. Over time, people start to see that you're here to stay and that builds confidence.

Some of my clients didn't hire me for over a year after we met. I kept showing up and staying in touch and eventually they had a need for what I do. At that moment, it was an easy decision to contact me.

If I didn't keep up my blog, maintain my relationships, and just generally showing up, I wouldn't get anywhere.

Angelique Rewers: Do it. And do it now, not later. It doesn't get easier if you wait. You'll never have all the pieces in place. And you can't get time back.

Amy Harrison: Don't limit your goals and dreams and be careful who you listen to. Even well-meaning friends and family might try and put you off your plans because they're concerned about you not making it. Also, don't wait too long to jump in and do it. You'll be surprised at how quickly you can overcome obstacles when you have to!

Barbara Milgram: To learn to love the fact that both success and failure rests squarely on your own shoulders. Know that nothing lasts forever — good or bad times — so remain agile and stay connected to other people. Working as a solopreneur shouldn't mean being disconnected: others are important to your sanity and success, so work hard to keep connections with others strong and solid.

Bill Dwight: Be determined to succeed, but be prepared to fail. Maybe it's the engineer in me, but always have a backup plan so you don't leave those who depend upon you in the lurch.

Laura Petrolino: If you are going to do it, do it all the way. Take the leap and devote all you have to your business and its development. It is very hard to be a part-time solopreneur. Get yourself to a point that you can go at it full tempo and go for it!

Also, never stop learning; budget your time so you learn something daily that can help your business, or sharpen or expand your skills. As a solopreneur you always have to be one step ahead. A constant focus on expanding your knowledge base will help this become a reality.

Dawn Svenson Holland:

1. Buy the book/take the Strengths Finder 2.0 test and reflect on what you learn in terms of the amazing, wonderful, unique value that only you bring to the world.

2. Follow your gut instinct, that inner voice, however it comes to you.

3. Find a formal or informal advisory group and always be open to the new perspectives they bring. Give back in the same manner.

4. Find an outlet that isn't truly related to your business and actively pursue it for new perspective and a chance to reflect.

Heather Claus: Get a good network. I not only have a great network of clients and partners locally, I am also active in the Third Tribe forums, and the advice is invaluable.

Laura Brandenburg: Get out and talk to your customers. And listen. My business model and career direction changed several times in my first year as an independent consultant. It was by talking to people and listening to what they needed and would pay for and then meshing that up with what I could deliver that I found a solid direction. I had to let go of a lot of ideas I was excited about simply because the market-place wouldn't support them.

It's also important to experiment. I started writing "How to Start a Business Analyst Career," my first eBook, simply because I had a bit of extra time on my hands. I had no idea this would be the foundation for me turning a blog into a product and set me up for other product releases.

Finally, make strategic decisions to automate and outsource. I spent the first 14 months sending my eNewsletter via an Outlook/Word mail merge with a manual sign-up process that I managed in an Outlook contact list. Looking back, I would have saved a lot of time choosing an e-mail provider early on, but I also probably would have chosen a provider that didn't meet the longer-term needs of bridging the gap. When I shifted to MailChimp, my subscribers started to grow exponentially and I opened up all kinds of new e-mail marketing opportunities. I still think I did this at exactly the right time and made the best possible decision about the product. Sometimes delaying the obvious decisions is strategic.

Similarly, decisions to outsource are also strategic. I chose my bookkeeper because she was also strong in social media. Because of this, I've been able to leverage her virtual assistance capabilities to help sustain the business. It's been possible to take small steps so I can learn how to outsource and not put myself into a position of negative cash flow.

Underlying the above advice is the reality that as a solopreneur, your personal and professional growth constrains the growth of your business. You need to be self-aware of your own abilities and limitations to keep the business growing but not beyond your control. I think this is a primary difference between solopreneurs and entrepreneurs.

Koldo Barroso: Don't listen to other people's advice too much, not even mine. Personally, I follow my own path.

Deb Howard Greenleaf: Do your homework! Understand what client problem you're trying to solve. What's their pain? You're selling solutions, not products and services. Also be sure to research what your first-year costs are going to be and how you're going to make ends meet until you hit break-even!

Natalia Sylvester: Don't let yourself get overwhelmed by the big picture. Focus on the small steps, put everything you've got into them, and they'll turn into something bigger before you know it.

Bob Andelman: Believe in yourself and pursue your dreams but first, always be willing to do whatever it takes to keep the lights on and your family fed.

Jill Chivers: Love it, learn it. You must be passionate about your area because you'll need that fire to keep you going during the tougher times. You also need to continue to "sit in the students chair" and be continually learning. Never assume you have hit the end of the learning road – there's always more to take on board.

Kelly Kingman: Start testing your ideas right now. Go find one client — don't worry about the perfect Web site or business cards (unless you design Web sites and business cards). Cobble together a modest portfolio of free projects you've done for people and go pitch somebody.

Also, experiment with your pricing and practice asking for more than you're totally comfortable with.

Laurie Gay: The best thing you can do is have fun with this — oh, and don't quit. Set yourself up so that you can enjoy creating your very own, totally special and awesome career without the incredible stress of falling into debt, worrying about money or what "everyone" might think.

That said, don't have a true backup plan (because if you have a true backup plan, that's really your plan) and have some accountability, either through a coach, a business partner or a friend (if "friend," choose one that you're kind of scared of so you'll actually follow through with what she's holding you to).

Tommy Walker: Don't ever quit! The amount of sacrifice and hard work you have to put in to make things work can be very exhausting. My first year I made less than $10,000 and that would seem like enough to stop anyone in their tracks. But don't! And listen to your instincts, don't sell out on your vision because someone else wants you to. Too often solopreneurs get an offer that they'll bend on what they do, just to find themselves in a moral conflict down the road. Don't! You can't afford to lose your spark.

Shayna Walker: Read, network, try and fail; it amounts to seeking as much education in your field and in business as you can, developing more connections than you could possibly ever conceive of needing, being open to new experiences and banishing a fear of failure. Read, network, try and fail.

Sherice Jacob: Running your business takes self discipline and hard work, especially in the beginning. Don't let anyone tell you that you can sit around in your pajamas and push buttons to make a living. You've got to work at it, but the experience is invaluable. I'd also advise getting a mentor if you feel stuck. You don't even have to pay them. Many of my mentors don't know that they are my mentors, but I watch what they write about, how they grow their business and try to follow in their footsteps while creating my own path.

Tricia Lawrence: Believe in your dream and commit to it 100%. Give yourself time; don't think you have to accomplish it all in one year or two. You've got time. Don't quit your day job if you can possibly hold on to it for a bit. Try moonlighting as an entrepreneur if at all possible. Bootstrap your entrepreneurial dreams and use your employment to fund your dreams. That said, it may be best for some to quit the job and launch out there, but you have to do what feels right for you. I did that back in 1995 and I learned so much. It was good for me. Now, I would not do the same thing. Of course, I have a mortgage to pay now, so perhaps I like living in a house too much.

Cindy Tonkin: Be clear on what your limits are, what you want, why you want it, and when you stop — celebrate.

Amy Pryor: Be organized with the business early; the longer you stay disorganized, the harder it will be to get organized. Embrace social media completely. The more research I do, the more I realize people do not want to talk on the phone. Besides, Facebook and Twitter are incredibly cheap ways to market. You can't get any cheaper than free. Don't worry so much about finding fans. Worry more about writing good content and offering a good product so people find you.

Helen Robinett: Build a network that will become your board room to thrash out the issues that you need serious assistance with.

Jim Sheard: Don't be in a hurry to give up your "day job" until you have the skills and expertise to proceed on your own. Listen to the advice of people who can coach you in the areas you do not know.

Patrick Curtis: Become an expert in a very narrow niche and serve that niche better than anyone else. Whether that is a blog and/or community, don't worry the form it takes, but do add value before trying to sell anything. It has taken me four years to get the business where it is today. If you are looking to make money without work, don't bother. If you are looking to make money on your own terms, be excited to wake up every morning and you are passionate about your business, then go for it!

Also, stop waiting and just start something today

(anything you are passionate about). It can be related to a hobby, work, anything. The worst that can happen is you fail; with the cost of starting something online so low nowadays, the only real risk is hurting your ego and learning a lot about yourself so you can execute better on your next venture.

Revka Stearns: Don't give up, and don't wait for perfection. There is so much to learn that you can get overwhelmed before you even begin. Be persistent. But don't be a perfectionist because that's an impossible goal. Perfectionism will keep you from taking those small steps that add up and will eventually take you where you want to go.

Tzaddi Gordon: 1. Make friends with your "competition." Maybe start out by working for them, as I did. You will learn so much from each other and build such a stronger network that way. Ideally you'll be different enough from each other that you're not really competitors anyway. Even if you're one of thousands who do "X" generally, you're YOU. The people you should be working with will gravitate toward you or a competitor naturally.

2. Become great at networking in whatever form makes sense for you. It could be in social media or blogging, or at live events. Build a strong network (not necessarily a big one). Your network is your business's lifeblood in so many ways.

Angelique Rewers: Do it. And do it now, not later. It doesn't get easier if you wait. You'll never have all the pieces in place. And you can't get time back.

Linda Lopeke: Before you do anything else, give yourself permission to succeed.

Stay your authentic course. Do not hang out with negaholics. Be impeccable with your word and, above all, no matter what happens, just keep moving forward. That's all you have to do. Practice persistence; build resilience. Every day remind yourself: perfection is NOT the goal; excellence will be tolerated. (My other favorite mantra is "this too will pass.")

Kelly Newsome: In no order:

1. Create a true, unconditional community/tribe of supporters.

2. Get daily goodness from blogs/books that keep

you motivated (I like Jonathan Fields, Chris Guillebeau, Pam Slim, and Pema Chodron).

3. Trust your instincts.

4. Keep a notebook at all times for random ideas, thoughts, conversations, and inspiration.

5. Make lots of to-do lists, preferably in said notebook; focus on the "A" and "B" priority items.

6. Remember that you'll want to quit. More than once. When that happens, follow steps 1-5 again.

Andy Hayes: If you spend enough time, you'll soon realise that most gurus have conflicting advice. But most of these people are successful, so if they say it worked, it worked for them. The real magic is figuring out what will work for YOU. Got to roll up those sleeves, little grasshopper!

Melissa Dinwiddie: Start. Just start. Take one step toward your goal, now. Don't let your fear that it's not perfect get in your way. Better to get something out there and tweak it, than labor over it forever and never ship! Most of all, follow your passions, but be prepared to work hard! It won't feel so much like work if you're doing what you love, but you do have to put the effort in.

Chapter 10
If You Were Starting Over, What Would You Do Differently?

Revka Stearns: I think I probably would have worked to surround myself with like-minded people who had been down the solopreneur road before and could give me a helping hand when needed.

I would say I'm the stereotypical solopreneur who feels she has to do everything herself. Now that I'm in a position where I can bring on additional help and where I've made business friends who listen and give advice when needed, I can see how having that support system in place from the beginning would have helped me get farther faster.

Ted Prodromu: I would focus on a small niche, work on PR to get my name/expertise out there and build recurring revenue into my business model.

Helen Robinett: Have more systems in place more quickly. Charge for what I gave away for free. Oh dear!

Jim Sheard: I would go to more school conferences, kids' events, and get home from work earlier, if at all possible. I would tell more people, especially my family, how much I appreciate (love) them.

Kelly Newsome: Educationally, I probably would've done a joint MBA/JD program, instead of just law school (mostly for the connections with other like-minded people). I would've also lived simply sooner — I wasted a lot of money on nonessentials in my early days. There are 273 more things I could've done differently, but that really is your education. For me, the lessons annihilate the regrets.

Sherice Jacob: Oh good question! The Internet is so different now than when I started. It's much more mainstream. I would have probably started networking with people a lot sooner. I'm just now seeming to come out of my "starving artist" shell and realize my full potential as a designer and writer. Don't let anyone tell you what they think you're worth or what you should charge. You'll eventually find a spot where you're comfortable. Then there's nowhere to go but UP!

Shayna Walker: There are advertising choices and product development that I wouldn't have pursued which would have saved me a lot of money.

I probably wouldn't have secured the office space that I did for three years which didn't result in an increase in income as I'd hoped.

I would have read my phone contract more closely (stuck for years!) and probably wouldn't have contracted for a merchant credit card terminal when there were other suitable and less expensive options.

There are people I wouldn't have trusted, and others whom I would have worked harder to know.

Lots of little things, but most of them were simply learning experiences and I am definitely a better business person having gone through them first-hand.

Diana Guerrero: Wow, this is hard to answer because on one hand, I would not change anything because of the valuable things I've learned and the unique experiences I've had.

If I knew then what I know now and could go back? I'd be more aggressive online earlier (I was up and running back in 1995) and would have made a few different choices on what battles I fought and how I prepped for my future. I also might have pursued the publishing and writing aspects of my career more aggressively.

Marianne Cantwell: Not much — maybe quit my second job (at Disney's European head offices) earlier. I'm not saying that because I loved every step of my career — quite the opposite, I was deeply unhappy for a lot of my "corporate cage" life. The thing is, I love where I am now. And it was the mix of experiences — working in media, then consulting — that laid the ground for where I am today. If everything had felt right and fallen into place from the start then I wouldn't appreciate what I have now! And I certainly wouldn't be passionate enough to dedicate myself to helping others escape the corporate cage — and that's not something I want to give up. So all in all, I feel pretty lucky!

Angelique Rewers: If I could start all over from the beginning I would chose a career path other than one that involves marketing, copywriting, business consulting etc. While I do love it, it requires A LOT of energy, creativity, brainpower, and hard work.

Dawn Svenson Holland: I would worry less about the amount of hours I put in and more about the quality of my work product. I would study and appreciate personality styles earlier and in more detail, both in general and as they apply to philanthropy. This was not something available to me through standard high school and college curriculum. I believe it's at the core of appreciating the value each individual brings.

David Billings: I wouldn't have worried so much about trying to fit in. I would have rocked the boat more, earlier on.

I used to worry so much about losing a job and not having the security of a paycheck. Now I have a new perspective of what security really is. I'll always find a way to support my family, so it's better to risk being who I am and handling things in the best way I know.

Patrick Curtis: Nothing. Working 100-hour weeks in investment banking and then getting fired after six months in private equity is exactly what inspired me to create Wall Street Oasis. I was young, overworked, and naïve — a common problem for aspiring "financiers." Sometimes getting your butt kicked can teach you a lot. Coming out of college, the earlier you realize life really is not fair the better off you'll be accepting the challenges ahead.

Amy Harrison: I'd have told myself not to worry so much and to trust that by working hard for my clients and working hard to build relationships, things would be O.K. and evolve at their own happy pace.

Chapter 11
Are You Glad You Became a Solopreneur?

Bob Andelman: I can't imagine doing anything but being self-employed. I like the freedom of setting my own hours, choosing who I will — or won't — work with on a daily basis, and being able to try different things on a moment's notice.

Deb Howard Greenleaf: Glad? You bet! The flexibility in my schedule has been a lifesaver and being my own boss makes me feel 10 years younger. I actually look forward to going to work now!

Laurie Gay: Most definitely. I'm not gonna lie, people — it's much more complicated and stressful than I imagined because you are every, single department (accounting, marketing, administration) and you will not be all that great at every one of these departments. But, the ups and downs and tremendous learning curve are really worth it: making money and finding real success doing something that is close to your true identity, that you created out of thin air, is the best feeling I have ever known. In business.

Natalia Sylvester: I couldn't be happier. It has its ups and downs, but so does any job. Becoming a solopreneur was one of the best decisions I ever made because it made me realize that I'm in charge of my life. That's a very empowering thing.

Marianne Cantwell: Hell yes! Oh my, imagine going to work every day with the commute and the office and the "holiday form" you have to fill out if you want to escape the cage. I felt like — in Studs Turkel's words — "a Monday to Friday sort of dying"... so yes I am very glad that now I can breathe and contribute a whole lot more to the world in the process.

Laura Brandenburg: Yes, definitely. It's given me the freedom to pursue my own career direction and broaden my experiences not just within my profession but also by building a business. You really can't underestimate what you learn when you go into business for yourself.

Patrick Curtis: Absolutely 100%. I just moved down to Buenos Aires. Why? Because I felt like getting my Spanish back and traveling. Working for someone else would not have given me this freedom. I can work when I want to work. If I am focused on something and I put in a 15-hour day, great. If I am tired and only want to do a 1 hour day or travel for a week, that also works.

Koldo Barroso: I'm glad that I realized that, being the way I am, in this particular moment it's good for me to be a solopreneur. I really don't care if I'm a solopreneur or not as long as I can be honest and true to my audience and my career. For some reason, so far nobody has opened their doors to me in this direction, except for my audience. So I'm happy to find a way to make it work like this.

On a different page, I also work in a different business with my wife, Naomi Niles, and I feel really happy about that too.

Amy Harrison: Definitely. I love the freedom and I love working on projects and for clients that truly get me fired up. When you land a new client, get good feedback or make great connections with other solopreneurs, it's just amazing.

Barbara Milgram: Absolutely. I love the freedom to plan my day based on workload, my own mood or anything else. I also appreciate that I'm the person responsible for making things happen, in both good and bad times.

There is a downside, however. I love collaborating with others and miss the energy and juice I get from working closely with other people. Sometimes I go to a coffee shop just to feel some human energy!

Bill Dwight: I'm ecstatic. I'm learning a ton. I'm pursuing my passions. I'm working with good friends. And, I'm able to work from home. This last one has two key benefits: I'm able to enjoy flexible time with my family, and my kids are able to observe my work (and my work ethic) firsthand.

David Billings: It's the best thing I ever did in my career. It's also the hardest thing I've ever done. I love being responsible for my own success or failure. When a client sends me a love note, I get to celebrate. When I screw something up, there's no one to blame but me. Either way, it's all my roller-coaster ride.

Dawn Svenson Holland: I am blessed beyond measure taking this leap of faith because I am being pushed out of my comfort zone in areas like learning to be an accountant. Although in some ways life is crazier than ever, because I am in control of my schedule, this is the first time in my career I feel like I have taken true steps towards life in the right priority order.

Diana Guerrero: Yes, mostly because of the freedom and lifestyle. I have a flexible schedule and time to live life. I also enjoy being able to be creative and innovative which has been threatening to others when I worked in the traditional work force.

Kelly Newsome: Yes. It's been one of the biggest challenges I've ever undertaken, and one of the best confidence-builders. It reminds me of when I was traveling around the world: you've got this map and some directions that may or may not be appropriately translated into your language, and you're just out there. You go forward, you walk, or you get lost. Sometimes both. And every time you make it to your destination, there's this feeling of success, relief, purpose, freedom, energy. You're exhausted, but you're usually exhausted from doing fiercely cool stuff.

Heather Claus: Yes. I'm no good at being an employee.

Melissa Dinwiddie: Honestly, I am not suited to being an employee! I haven't had a "real job" for over 20 years and I don't think I could go back. I love working at home, setting my own hours, creating what I want to create. So yes, I love being a solopreneur, and I'm excited to see how my business evolves!

Shayna Walker: I have learned so many life lessons, and so much about myself from this solopreneur adventure that I'm definitely glad. It has not been an easy path, but it has been rewarding in so many ways.

I may not stay "solo" for life, but for this round it's a perfect place to be.

Sherice Jacob: YES! I wouldn't trade it for anything. I don't have to answer to anyone but myself — and I'm tougher on myself than any boss I've had ever was. It keeps me, and my work, up to a higher standard.

Tommy Walker: Absolutely! I do things on my terms, work with people that I choose and who will not question my advice, only challenge me to do better.

Tricia Lawrence: I am so glad I became a solopreneur. It fits my personality perfectly. Even though I appear on paper as a full-blown corporation, it's just me and I love it. Sure, I have a to-do list that is way too long and sometimes I burn out on my own dreams, but I would burn out so much faster on someone else's dreams.

Jill Chivers: Yes! Having worked in corporate land for many years, and then seeing it through the eyes of workshop participants who attended my programs, I couldn't work full time as an employee in that environment again. I'm happily unemployable!

I love having my own schedule; some days this means I work only a couple of hours, and other days it means I work long after it's gotten dark. I feel very blessed to be living this life.

Jill Salzman: ABSOLUTELY. I find that explaining the joys of solopreneurship are akin to trying to explain why one likes chocolate. Because.

Kelly Kingman: Absolutely! I will never go back to asking for time off — I'm completely in control of my time. I love it.

Helen Robinett: Oh you bet I am. I get to choose. My life has a balance of my not-for-profit work, family, business, and some fun. It works. It fuels me and brings a great level of peace.

Jim Sheard: To retire early to do this was one of the great blessings of my life. I am glad I did not have live off of what I was able to earn doing it.

Revka Stearns: I love being a solopreneur. It's satisfying to have my own business and to watch it grow and flourish as I learn more. I love being able to help people who are where I was only a few short years ago. I love having the freedom to decline work that doesn't suit me. I love being able to contribute financially so that my family can do and have some "extra" things — like going to concerts, attending Broadway productions, and taking a short family vacation each year.

I'd rather share experiences with my family than purchase more things — things get thrown in the trash; experiences are stored in our memories forever.

Burton Kelso: I am very happy that I took the leap. Although everyone faces professional challenges, I believe solopreneurs face an even bigger uphill battle. You have a great sense of achievement when you are able to meet those challenges head on and conquer them.

Achievement gives you swagger and swagger gives you the confidence to get out there and get what's yours — which is the ability to achieve your dreams.

Nichole Bazemore: Absolutely. Working for myself has forced me to trust myself. It's forced me to push through my fears and in the process, I've become bolder and more empowered in other areas of my life.

Shannon Reece: I couldn't be happier being a solopreneur! I spent many years working hard for other people's dreams. It took getting kicked out of my comfort zone to get me to finally pursue my own, and I haven't looked back.

Starting a business was very challenging, with a steep learning curve. And frankly, you never stop learning as you go. But there is a huge difference between labor for someone else, and a labor of love as you fulfill your purpose in life.

Melissa Dinwiddie: Honestly, I am not suited to being an employee! I haven't had a "real job" for over 20 years and I don't think I could go back. I love working at home, setting my own hours, creating what I want to create. So yes, I love being a solopreneur, and I'm excited to see how my business evolves!

Angelique Rewers: Absolutely. I can't imagine doing things any differently. I once had a friend say to me, "well if you hit a rough patch you could always get a job." There was a visceral reaction in my stomach when I heard that. I knew then that under no circumstance would I ever have a J.O.B. again.

Tzaddi Gordon: YES! I love to learn and do meaningful work. As a solopreneur I'm doing both every day, even with tasks that might not feel like it on the surface. It's extremely satisfying to help people follow their dreams and make the world a better place.

About the Editor

Larry Keltto, the co-author of *Relationship Marketing for Solopreneurs: How to Build Rewarding Connections in Work and Life*, is founder and publisher of TheSolopreneurLife.com, an online resource for solopreneurs. Larry has been a solopreneur since 1993; he specializes in providing marketing, communications, and coaching services to small businesses. He lives in Owatonna, Minnesota with his wife and two daughters.